Contents

Acknowledgements
Text by John Shedden (skiing) and Steve Ensor (snowboarding).
The publishers would like to thank Salomon Ski Equipment Ltd for their photographic contributions to this book.

Photographs on cover from Jump; inside front cover and pages 2, 3, 7, 14, 18, 21, 25, 26, 27, 30, 35, 37, 42 from Action Plus; photographs on inside back cover and pages 36, 41, 45, 46 from Steve Ensor (Slip and Slide).
Illustrations by Jones Sewell & Associates, Dave Saunders and Steve Ensor.

Note Throughout the book skiers are referred to individually as 'he'. This should, of course, be taken to mean 'he or she' where appropriate.

Skiing

Introduction

The sport of skiing is enjoyed by millions of people all over the world. It is one of the few activities in which age is not a barrier to participation. Children as young as three or four years of age enjoy the exhilaration of skiing alongside their parents and even their grand-parents.

Whether you are planning a visit to an artificial slope or to a mountain resort, your safety, progress, enjoyment and value for money will be dependent on preparing yourself fully for the excitement ahead.

The English Ski Council

Area Library Building
Queensway Mall
The Cornbow
Halesowen
West Midlands B63 4AJ

Tel: 0121 501 2314
Fax: 0121 585 6448
E-mail: esc@tesco.net

Fitness

Skiing is a physically demanding activity. In order to be able to learn new and alien techniques correctly the muscles of the body must be strong and supple. High levels of stamina will ensure that the skier will be able to delay the onset of fatigue that could force him to leave the slopes, or even face the possibility of an accident through overtiredness. Circuit training is a great method of improving both strength and stamina levels.

First warm up by jogging on the spot, by stepping from foot to foot, and by circling the arms. Then practise the following exercises to ensure that you are able to perform them correctly, and incorporate them into your personal fitness regime.

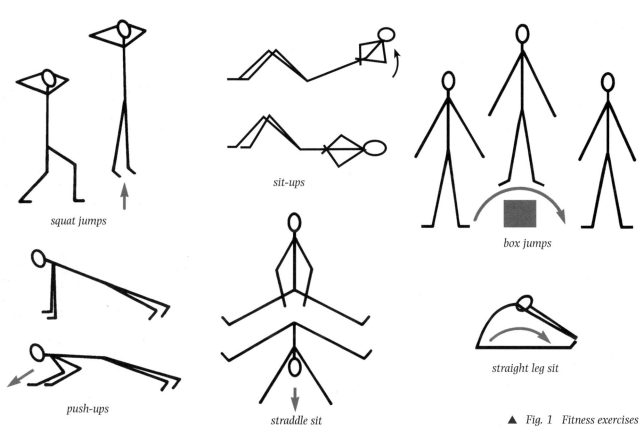

squat jumps

sit-ups

box jumps

push-ups

straddle sit

straight leg sit

▲ Fig. 1 Fitness exercises

4

Squat jumps

Stand with one foot in front of the other. Jump into the air, changing feet as you do so. Land in a squat. Repeat.

Sit-ups

Sit on the floor, legs bent and arms folded. Roll back on to the floor, then return to the starting position without lifting your feet.

Box jumps

Place an empty crisp box (or something similar) on a non-slippery floor. Jump over the box, taking off and landing on two feet.

Push-ups

Support yourself on your hands, fingers facing forwards. Lower your chest and chin to the floor. Return to the starting position, trying to keep the body straight.

Your personal circuit

When you are confident that you can perform the exercises correctly, test the maximum number of repetitions you can manage of each exercise in a minute. (Take a rest between each test.)

Record your score on a performance sheet. Then divide the score for each exercise by two to determine your training load – the number of repetitions of each exercise you will perform in the circuit. Now you are ready to complete a circuit. Begin with squat jumps, then sit-ups, box jumps and push-ups. Rest for up to two minutes after one set of exercises in order to recover. Repeat two more circuits, with a rest in between each.

Replace the following examples with your own score.

	Squat jumps	Sit-ups	Box jumps	Push ups
Test	32	26	34	8
Training	16 (x3)	13 (x3)	17 (x3)	4 (x3)

Aim to do three training sessions a week for three or four weeks. Then retest the maximum number of repetitions that you are able to perform in a minute.

In addition to circuit training, walking, jogging, cycling and swimming will help to improve your levels of stamina. Maintain the effort for at least 30 minutes without stopping to rest.

Flexibility

Suppleness of the leg and hip muscles will aid you in learning skiing techniques. It will also contribute to a reduction in the stiffness experienced after skiing, and help to lessen the risk of injury from falls.

Straddle sit

Sit on the floor, legs straight and at right angles. Bend forward as far as you can. Hold the position for 10 to 15 seconds, and try to relax. Bend forwards a little more and hold again for 10 to 15 seconds.

Straight leg sit

Sit on the floor, legs straight and ankles together. Reach forwards as far as you can. Hold the position for 10 to 15 seconds, and relax in this position. Reach forwards a little more and hold.

Repeat each exercise five times. To add more interest, measure how far you can reach the first time you do the exercises. Measure again after three or four weeks. You should see an improvement!

Clothing

Like many other sports, skiing is not without its hazards. The risk of injury can be reduced by ensuring that you wear the appropriate clothing.

Artificial slopes

Artificial slopes are usually made from fibrous bristles, making them feel rather like a scrubbing brush. The surface is very abrasive and can damage both your skin and your clothing if you fall.

However, an artificial slope is not the place to wear your new ski clothing; this is designed to keep you warm in the mountains. Instead, wear long sleeves and long trousers, no matter how hot the weather. A tracksuit is ideal, because unlike jeans it will not restrict your movement.

Substantial gloves are essential to protect your hands. A pair of sturdy gardening gloves is one of the best and cheapest alternatives.

Mountain slopes

In a mountain resort the problem is not so much one of protecting yourself from the skiing surface, as one of keeping dry and warm. Your clothing must create your own personal micro-climate, which will protect you from what may sometimes become a hostile environment. These are the basic items that you will need.

Hat

Made of wool or acrylic fibre. Must be large enough to cover your ears on very cold days.

Scarf

Made of cotton or silk to keep out the wind. Can also be used as a mask on 'bad' days.

Shirts

Cotton polo-neck shirts are ideal.

Ski jacket

Must be wind- and shower-proof. Should have a hood and high collar. Zip pockets will keep valuables safe if you fall. Remember to choose a size that will enable you to wear one or two sweaters underneath.

Sweaters

Two lightweight sweaters or sweat-shirts are better than one thick one.

Underwear

Thermal underwear and 'long johns' are essential in cold weather.

Trousers

'Salopettes' are preferable to ski pants because they are thoroughly wind- and shower-proof. They also extend further above the waist, keeping the lower back warm.

Socks

Have several pairs of knee-length ski socks at your disposal. Wear one clean pair for best fit and comfort.

Gloves/mitts

Good quality gloves or mitts are essential to keep your hands warm and dry. In addition to protecting yourself from the cold, it is essential to protect your skin and eyes from the intense levels of ultra-violet light experienced in the mountains. Wear sunglasses, or ski goggles with interchangeable lenses. Goggles are preferable because they are more sturdy.

Lip salve will help protect your lips from cold sores and cracking.

Skin cream with a protection factor of SPF 8 or higher is reasonable for low altitude and midwinter, while SPF 20 or higher is necessary in springtime or at high altitude.

Equipment

Ski equipment is expensive to buy. Unless you have been skiing before and intend to participate regularly, it is more sensible to hire your equipment as part of your holiday package.

Boots

Ski boots are the most important item of your equipment. Whether you decide to hire or buy them, you must ensure that they fit well so that your feet will be warm and comfortable. A correct fit will help you to control your skis.

Ski boots are made from plastic or polyurethane. These two materials enable the manufacturers to design boots which will limit dangerous lateral movement, but at the same time allow near normal bending and straightening of the ankle – an essential element of good technique. (It is a misconception of many skiers that they must 'bend the knees': in fact, they should first bend the ankles, which in turn causes the knees to bend.)

Skis

Modern skis are manufactured from a mixture of materials. They are classified according to their design characteristics and their suitability to the various levels of skiers' abilities. Beginners and intermediates do not need the same performance characteristics as advanced and competition skiers. Clearly the type of skis you hire or buy need to suit your individual needs. Always seek expert advice on this point: your experience, height and weight must be taken into consideration to ensure that you choose a pair of skis to match your requirements.

Shaped skis

Shaped skis represent over 90% of all skis sold. Their outstanding feature is ease of manoeuvrability. With a 96–110 mm (2.68–2.83 in) shovel width, they are slightly broader than other skis and, as a result, are easier to turn in new snow as well as on the compacted snow of the piste. They are excellent for learning new techniques and will suit both beginners and intermediate skiers, who should select chin-height skis. More experienced skiers, including advanced skiers, should choose skis from nose-height to just above head-height.

All modern skis are now classified as either Freeride skis or All-round carving skis.

Freeride skis are designed to perform off piste as well as on piste (piste is compacted snow).

All-round carving skis are designed for style and precision on piste.

Sport skis

Sport skis are similar in their construction to competition skis. They are, however, 'detuned', which means that the materials used are not as strong or firm, and therefore require less strength or speed from the skier to make them perform. Sport skis are suitable for intermediate and experienced skiers, who want precision as well as ease of turning in All-round carving skis.

Competition skis

Competition skis have specialised designs to meet the needs of competitive skiers in the slalom, giant slalom and downhill disciplines. Not surprisingly, they require the very precise steering and control shown by only the most experienced and advanced skiers. The length chosen is dependent on the discipline.

Freestyle skis

Freestyle skis have a specialised reinforced design to meet the demands of skiers in the freestyle disciplines of ballet, moguls and aerials. They are not suitable for beginners and intermediate skiers.

Edges

All modern skis have a continuous strip of metal running along the outside edges of their base. These are essential for control and ease of steering.

Ski bindings

Ski bindings perform two important functions: they attach the boot to the ski; and they are also designed to release the boot when it is subjected to twisting or forward forces during a fall, providing they are set on the correct DIN (Deutsche Industrie Normen) setting. This is vitally important for your safety and is determined for each individual by his age, weight, height and skiing ability. The DIN setting is marked on a graduated scale. This scale is normally from 2 or 3 to 10 or 12 on both the toe and the heel bindings; 2 is the lowest setting, with very little force required to open the bind-

ing; 12 is a very high setting, and makes the bindings extremely hard to release. Most recreational skiers, irrespective of their experience and ability, will require a setting in the middle of the range. If you are unsure that your binding is set correctly, seek expert guidance from your local ski shop, or from the hire shop if you have hired the equipment.

Ski brakes

Ski brakes are the spring-loaded prongs which prevent the skis from running away when you are not skiing on them.

Ski sticks

Ski sticks are made from lightweight metal alloy, fibreglass or plastic materials. While they are an important item of equipment for experienced skiers, they can be a nuisance for less accomplished skiers: many artificial ski slopes have dispensed with sticks for beginners. Ski shops in the mountain resorts will still continue to issue them as part of your hire package. If you do have them, remember the following:

- the height of the sticks should enable you to stand with your forearm parallel to the snow's surface when you are holding the stick vertically on level terrain
- the hand grip should be moulded to enable a comfortable grip, with a loop through which the hand passes from underneath to prevent you losing the sticks when you are skiing. These retention straps should not be used on an artificial slope
- the baskets at the pointed ends of the sticks prevent the sticks from sinking into the snow. The points of the sticks should be 'ice heads' (an ice head is the four-pointed or dished end of the ski stick) to increase the grip when the tip is in contact with the snow.

Maintenance of equipment

The ease with which you either learn or practise your newly acquired skill is in part dependent on the condition of your ski equipment. If it is your own equipment, you should service it yourself or have it serviced at your local ski shop before your holiday. If you are hiring the equipment, check that it is in good condition when it is issued to you. If it is not, insist on being given some that is!

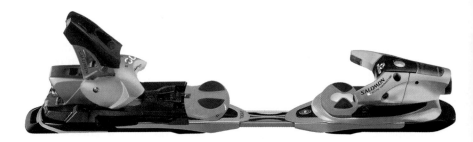

Check list

• Make sure that the bindings are working and that the DIN setting is correct for your weight and ability.

• Check that the bases of the skis are smooth. Any deep scratches or gouges will affect the steering and sliding characteristics of the skis. Damaged areas can normally be filled with a special polythene strip that is melted and dripped into the holes, then scraped smooth when it has hardened.

• Check that the ski bases are flat by placing a straight edge across them – make sure that you cannot see any light in between. (They may be slightly convex, but they must not be concave.)

• Make sure that the ski bases have been waxed. Ski wax prevents the bases drying out and improves their sliding ability. Advanced skiers apply different waxes, the exact requirement being determined by the snow temperature and texture. This is not necessary for beginners and intermediates, who will find that a rub-on or spray wax is adequate for their needs.

• Check that the edges are smooth, with no jagged areas. Also check that the edges are sharp by drawing a finger-nail across them. If they require either smoothing or sharpening, take them to the ski shop or do it yourself with a flat file and a specialist edge sharpener purchased from the ski shop. Do not sharpen the edges approximately 20 cm (8 in) from the top and tail because this will cause the skis to grip and over-steer.

• In addition to a daily check on your skis, it is advisable to put aside some time to make sure that your boots will continue to keep you warm and dry. There is nothing worse than putting on cold, wet boots at the start of a day's skiing. Wipe off any excess water before placing the boots in a rack in a warm room. Alternatively, take them back to your room. If you have detachable inner boots, take them out and dry them separately.

• Make sure that your clothing and gloves are placed somewhere to dry before you need them again. If you return to your hotel for lunch, you will be more comfortable if you take the trouble to dry any damp or wet clothes before the afternoon session.

First steps on skis

Until you are able to move around with confidence and in safety, you should rely on qualified ski school staff to teach you the basic techniques. Later, as your skill develops, you will be able to practise what you have learned with friends.

Your instructor should take you through most of the following drills and exercises to familiarise you with the equipment and what may seem at first to be awkward movements.

Carrying skis and sticks

Skis are carried on the shoulder, held together with rubber straps and interlocked ski brakes. They should point slightly downwards, with the ski tips forwards and the bindings resting just behind the shoulder. Take care to avoid knocking anyone or anything with the ends of the skis, especially when you are turning around. Ski sticks are carried in the other hand. In confined spaces and lift queues, it's easier and safer to carry your skis vertically in front of you.

Warm-up

Warming up is as important before skiing as it is before fitness training. Your routine should include running on the spot, hopping, and arm circling and swinging. Stop before you become hot; sweating cools the body, especially in the cold mountain air. Only warm up; skiing will keep you warm.

Putting on skis

Choose a flat piece of ground and place the skis side by side. First place the toe of one boot into the toe binding of one ski. Make sure that the boot is straight on the ski, then press the heel of the boot into the heel binding. Repeat for the second boot

If you have to put them on whilst on a slope, the skis must be placed horizontally. You will find it easier if you put on the ski nearest to the valley first.

Ski sticks

If you do have ski sticks for your first lesson, it is important to know how to use them. The hand should pass through the loop from underneath and then grip the stick over the loop. (Do not use these loops on dry slopes.) The sticks can be used to help you balance and to assist when you are climbing and turning. But do not rely on them excessively – it's easier just to use the skis correctly.

Moving on the flat

Before rushing off to enjoy the thrills of sliding down a slope, you need to learn how to move on a flat surface.

• Lift alternate skis while you are standing still.
• Hop the tails of the skis.
• Make wedge shapes, firstly by moving the tails of the skis apart and keeping the tips together to form an 'A' shape. Then move the tips apart while you keep the tails together, making a 'V' shape. The first shape is the 'wedge' or 'snowplough', one of the most important elements in skiing, and will form the basis for a great deal of your early learning.
• Turn to face another direction using 'clock turns' – small, angled, step movements – lifting and opening the tails of the skis and keeping the tips on the ground.
• To move forward on the flat, keep the skis flat, parallel and slightly apart. Bend your ankles and slide one ski forwards, then the other. Allow the skis to glide forwards at the end of each push. Try to keep both skis on the ground.

▲ *Fig. 2 Moving and turning on the flat*

13

Climbing

When you have practised all these manoeuvres, you will be almost ready for your first slide down the hill. First, however, you need to go up and then turn to face straight down the hill – the 'fall-line'.

Your instructor will choose an appropriate slope with a gentle gradient and a level run-out at the bottom so that you will stop easily. If at a later stage you practise on your own, be sure that you use the same nursery slope or one with the same shape.

There are two methods of walking up a hill on your skis:

- side-stepping: stepping sideways with the skis across the slope to prevent them sliding
- herring-bone stepping: walking straight up the slope with the skis in the 'V'-shaped wedge that you practised on the flat. To stop the skis sliding down, press the big toes into the ground so that the edges of the skis grip the snow or mat.

You now need to turn your skis so that they point down the hill. If you used the herring-bone step to climb up, you must first turn to stand with both skis across the slope. If you side-stepped, you will already be in the correct position.

Use the clock turn, the 'A'-shaped wedge that you learned on the flat. Step the tails of the skis around with small movements, gripping the slope with the inside edges of the skis.

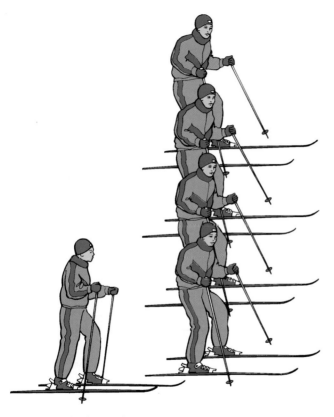

*ski tips open
in wide 'V'*

*repeat first step and
continue climbing*

*weight on right ski:
step up left ski*

*stand on left ski:
step up right ski*

*both skis against
inside edge*

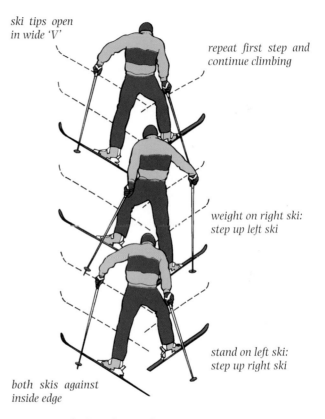

▲ *Fig. 3 Climbing: side-stepping*

▲ *Fig. 4 Climbing: herring-bone stepping*

Schussing

When you are facing down the slope, flatten the skis and allow them to slide. Keep your feet hip width apart and allow your weight to press down on the entire length of both feet to help you balance.

Repeat the climbing, turning and sliding routine until you are confident that you can do it easily. Now you are ready to try some other exercises.

Instead of making a clock turn to face down the hill, try jumping both skis around using either small or large jumps.

As you slide down, steer your skis straight and keep them parallel. Then during consecutive descents:

● lift one foot, then the other;
● bend down to touch your toes, then stretch up tall;
● hop the heels of the skis off the ground;
● shuffle your feet so that first one foot then the other moves about a boot-length forwards.

After several straight descents, when you feel confident, instead of just allowing your skis to stop on the flat, step the tips of the skis around to the left or right so that you are facing across the slope before you stop. Remember to practise this to both sides.

adopt a high, relaxed posture, legs slightly flexed

▲ *Fig, 5 Schussing*

As your confidence increases, try the same stepping manoeuvre as you descend the slope. Change direction as you slide down by making a small hop to one side.

lean forwards to counteract inertia and the acceleration of the skis, and to stay in contact with the snow

▲ *Fig. 6 Schussing: descending a slope*

Skiing in a wedge or snowploughing

The next challenge is to ski down the slope with your skis in the 'A'-shaped wedge or snowplough. This will enable you to control your speed, and later to steer and control your direction of travel.

Start with your skis in the wedge shape, and allow them to skid down the slope. Crouch down slightly and bend your legs, then push your feet apart and the heels out to maintain the 'A' shape. Keep the ski tips about 20 cm (8 in) apart to avoid them crossing over. Push your skis apart but avoid stiffening your legs. Feel that your weight is distributed along the whole length of each foot, from your big toe to the inside of your heel.

Practise straight descents in the fall-line until you feel comfortable and confident in your ability to influence your speed. Then attempt the following exercises.

- While retaining the wedge shape, crouch down and then stand taller.
- Vary the width of the wedge. You will notice that this movement will influence your speed – the smaller the angle, the greater the speed.
- Make small hopping movements with the tails of the skis.
- Start down the slope with the skis parallel, crouch slightly and then brush them out into an 'A'-shaped wedge, and then back to parallel again. Repeat this manoeuvre with a regular rhythm, allowing yourself to go up and down like a spring.

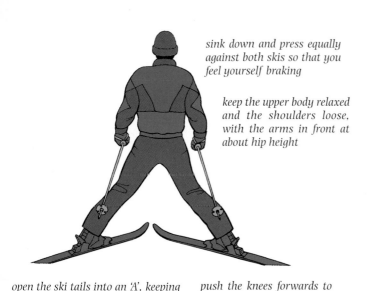

sink down and press equally against both skis so that you feel yourself braking

keep the upper body relaxed and the shoulders loose, with the arms in front at about hip height

open the ski tails into an 'A', keeping the ski tips slightly apart

push the knees forwards to tilt the skis into the snow, against their inside edges

▲ *Fig. 7 The snowplough*

with the skis parallel and flat on the snow, and in a high stance, ski straight down the fall-line

sink down and push your skis out into a slight wedge or 'A' shape, against their inside edges

push against your skis so you feel them control your speed

stay low and steer your skis parallel – keep them apart

as your skis move parallel again, you will feel your speed increasing

fall-line

▲ *Fig. 8 Snowploughing to control speed*

Steering

Turning as you descend the slope is achieved by resisting your forward motion, i.e. 'gripping' slightly, with one ski more than the other. Press against your right ski (down into the snow) and allow it to grip by continuing to resist your forward motion a little. This will turn you to the left; pressing against the left ski will turn you to the right.

Make a descent, linking the turns together rhythmically.

Vary the width of the 'A' shape and also the extent to which you turn. As you grow in confidence, turn more so that you travel across the slope between each turn. Allow the inner ski to move parallel to the downhill (or outer) ski as you travel across the slope. Brush or step the uphill ski again into the plough shape to make the next turn.

It may help to concentrate on the tips of your skis: close the tips to make the wedge; open the tips to make the skis parallel. Practise the movement standing on level ground before you attempt it on the slope.

Test the accuracy of your steering and turning by skiing around markers placed on the slope, or better still by aiming at markers placed down the sides of your ski run.

▼ *Fig. 9 Steering*

keep the body centred between the skis

steer with the knees and the feet, not with the shoulders

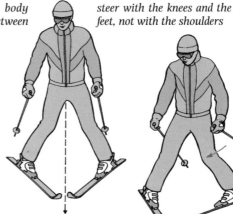

flex your right knee and push against your right big toe to steer to your left

if you weight and edge both skis equally, you will snowplough straight down the fall-line

flex your left knee and push against your left big toe to steer to your right

begin your motion in the fall-line, your skis equally weighted and ploughing

sink down slightly and press against your left big toe to steer to your right

return to neutral and then press against your right big toe to steer to the left

while changing direction, try to develop a series of rhythmically steered turns

do the steering with your legs and feet, and keep your upper body calm and loose; you should generally 'face' the way you are going, i.e. downhill

◄ *Fig. 10 Linking the turns*

21

Falling over

All skiers fall over. Being aware of what to do when you fall greatly reduces the possibility of any injury.

- When you feel yourself falling, sit down to the side of your skis.
- Before you touch the ground, *extend* your legs and keep doing so until you have stopped moving.
- Keep your hands clear of the snow or matting.

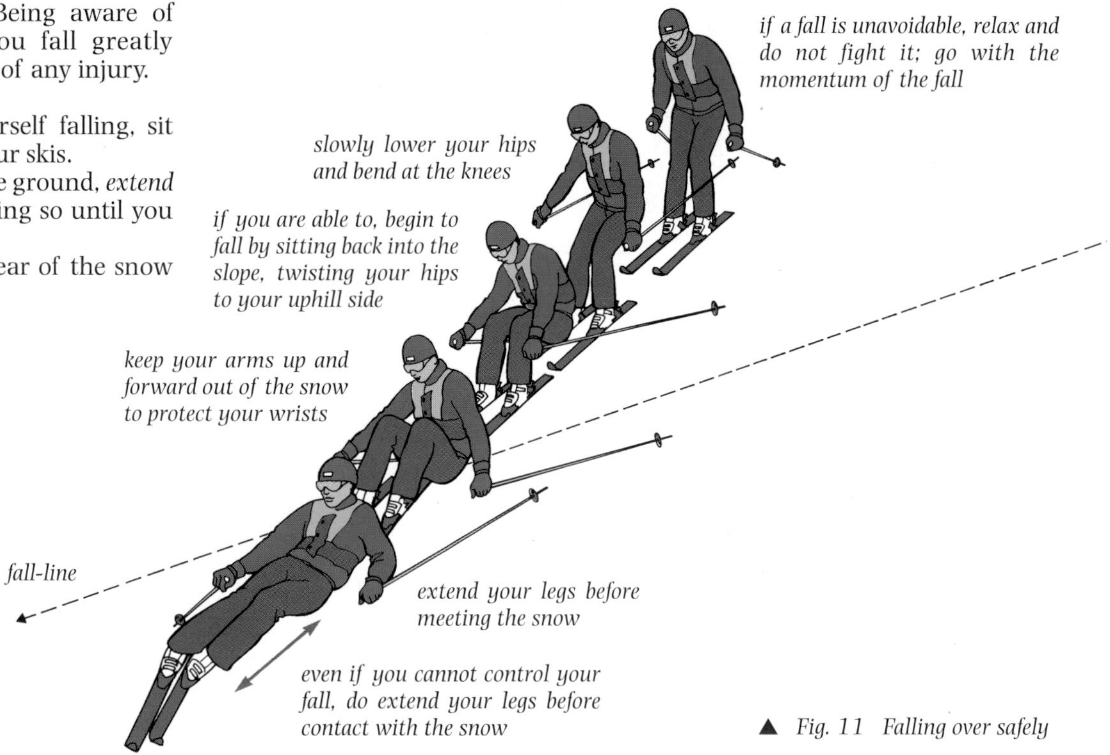

if a fall is unavoidable, relax and do not fight it; go with the momentum of the fall

slowly lower your hips and bend at the knees

if you are able to, begin to fall by sitting back into the slope, twisting your hips to your uphill side

keep your arms up and forward out of the snow to protect your wrists

fall-line

extend your legs before meeting the snow

even if you cannot control your fall, do extend your legs before contact with the snow

▲ *Fig. 11 Falling over safely*

Getting up

- First move both skis so that they are downhill from your body and across the slope.
- Next, sit close to your heels.
- Push the lower ski further away from your body, roll your knees above your feet, pull yourself forwards and stand up.
- If you find this too difficult, use your ski sticks to push yourself up.

▼ *Fig. 12 Getting up safely*

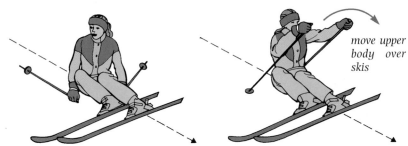

move upper body over skis

draw up the skis beneath the body at right angles to the fall-line

plant the sticks uphill on either side of the hips, close to the body

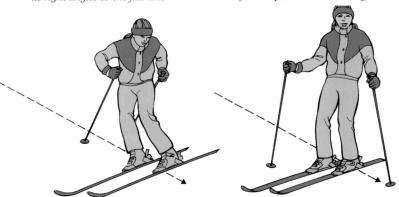

edge the skis, push off from both sticks and lever yourself up and on to your skis

keep the skis edged into the snow and stand straight upright

23

Tows and lifts

When you have mastered some or all of the basic techniques, your instructor will introduce you to the use of ski lifts, which are normally sited alongside the nursery slopes. Lifts reduce the hard work of walking up the slope and also allow you to spend more of your time practising the techniques of skiing down.

Tows and lifts vary in their design.

Rope tow

Simply hold the rope with both hands. Imagine it is a tug-of-war rope; try to pull the rope straight down the slope.

Bar lift

A rope tow with fixed plastic or metal handles.

Button lift

A metal pole with a button-shaped end.

T-bar

An anchor-shaped pole that is designed for use by two skiers. It is easier for beginners if they travel up with an experienced skier.

When using a ski lift, remember that it is designed to tow you up the hill. It will not hold you upright so you should not rely on it for balance.

Keep your skis hip-width apart as you are pulled up the hill; this is easier on snow than artificial slopes because you can follow the tracks made by other skiers. Do not make any turning movements.

When getting off the lift, step around out of the tow track and face across the slope to ensure you do not slip back down the slope. Move away from the lift as soon as you can to enable the skiers following you to get off easily.

If you fall over, scramble clear of the lift track as quickly as you can so that you do not pose a hazard for the skiers following you up.

In most ski resorts the nursery slopes are situated on the valley floor and are easily accessible from the hotels. However, if the snow in the valley is inadequate, as it can be early or late in the season, it may be necessary for your instructor to take your class higher on the mountain, using other forms of uphill transport to get up to the higher nursery slopes (including chair lifts, cable-cars, gondolas, funicular and cog railways).

When using lifts regularly, you will need a 'lift pass' – in effect, a season ticket. This is best carried around your neck on a piece of string (usually supplied) so that it is always handy to use and will not be lost or misplaced. Some ski resorts now use electronic tags which allow you to pass through the turnstyles without using your hands to operate the lift pass 'switch'.

keep the skis parallel in the tracks, both sticks in one hand

grab the bar and slip the button between your legs

as the bar starts moving, let it pull you forwards; 'shuffle' your feet a little to help the skis begin to slide

▲ *Fig. 13 Using the button lift*

Safety

While learning and practising the basic techniques, your instructor will have taken your class on terrain where you are comparatively safe. As your ability improves and your confidence grows, you may wish to ski with friends in an unsupervised group. But always remember that you must never venture on to slopes that are too steep and/or too difficult for you. As well as posing enormous dangers to your personal safety, such an experience would do little for either your confidence or your technique.

Ski slopes and ski runs, known as 'pistes', are graded and colour coded according to their level of difficulty.

• Green pistes are shallow and suitable for beginners.
• Blue pistes are quite shallow and are suitable for improving and intermediate level skiers.
• Red pistes are quite steep and sometimes narrow, and are suited to good skiers of several years' experience.
• Black pistes are the steepest and most difficult, and should only be attempted by expert or advanced skiers. The snow cover on black pistes is often very patchy, and rocks are frequently exposed; skiing on them may not only damage your skis, but also the delicate natural environment.

Pistes are shown on a resort map, known as a 'piste map', and are indicated on the mountain by coloured and numbered piste markers.

Ensuring that you ski only on pistes appropriate to your ability will contribute to your staying reasonably safe. In addition to the rather obvious need to ensure your own safety, you have a responsibility to do all that you can to avoid endangering your fellow skiers. What is expected of all skiers is contained in the 'International Skiway Code'.

The Skiway Code

To ski responsibly and safely demands skill on the part of the skier.

- A skier shall conduct himself in such a manner that he does not endanger others.
- A skier must ski in control and at a speed which is within his personal ability and which is appropriate to the terrain, weather and snow conditions.
- A skier coming from above (uphill) must choose a route that avoids skiers below.
- A skier may overtake another skier to the right or left, but he must give ample room for the other skier to make his turns.
- Look around, especially uphill, before joining a new ski run or piste, and before starting off again after a stop or fall.
- Avoid stopping at narrow places or below the crest of a ridge where you may not be seen by other skiers approaching from higher up the piste.
- Move out of the way as quickly as you can after a fall.

- Keep to the edge of the piste when you climb up on your skis or walk down on foot.
- Take notice of the signs warning you of dangers on the mountains. Some runs may be closed because of lack of snow or because there is a possibility of an avalanche. Other signs will indicate local hazards.
- If you come across an accident or an injured skier, give assistance by offering to inform someone. The personnel who work on ski lifts are usually able to summon help from the rescue services. They will need to know the approximate location of the casualty. Being able to mark the spot on a piste map is helpful.
- If you witness an accident you may be asked for your name and address, just as you would if you witnessed a motor accident at home. In such a case, be as helpful as you can.

Onwards and downwards

Having mastered the basics, your instructor will introduce you to the intermediate techniques.

Skidded turns

The swing to the hill or uphill turn will introduce you to skidded steering with the skis parallel. This is the main element of all advanced skiing.

Ski down the fall-line using a narrow plough. 'Open' the tip of one ski so that the skis are parallel; this will cause the skis to skid and turn away from the fall-line. At first, simply stand still on both feet with a relaxed upper body. You will continue diagonally across the slope for a short distance before stopping.

Practise this technique to both sides. As your confidence grows, start to steer the skis in the skid phase by simply turning your legs so that the tips of the skis point more towards the side of the piste. Again, practise this technique to both left and right.

Linked skidded turns

This is a simple progression from the previous exercise; it will introduce you to basic parallel turning.

- Start down the slope using a narrow plough.
- 'Open' the tip of one ski as before and start to skid with your skis parallel.
- Before you slow down, close the tips of the skis to reform your plough and steer downhill again.
- Then almost immediately 'open' the other tip and skid round to the other side.
- Keep the body slightly crouched, calm and loose as you make the turns.
- Vary the shape of your track or rhythm of your turns from wide swinging turns that take you away from the fall-line and slow you down, to faster turns at higher speeds closer to the fall-line on shallow slopes.

- Remember to feel for the resistance that your skis create – this controls your speed and direction.
- Remember that you can steer the skid by turning your legs to point the skis where you want them to go.
- Add rhythm to your skiing. Stand up slightly as you close the tips; sink down as you open them.
- Alter the timing of your movements so that as you close the tip of the outer ski, you lift the inner ski tip away from it. Your turning will become more fluent and easier to initiate as your stability increases and your confidence and speed grow.

Only move on to more difficult terrain when these movements are well established. The world's best skiers perfect their technique on quite shallow gradients before they attempt the more demanding slopes. They practise these basic movements every season before the racing begins.

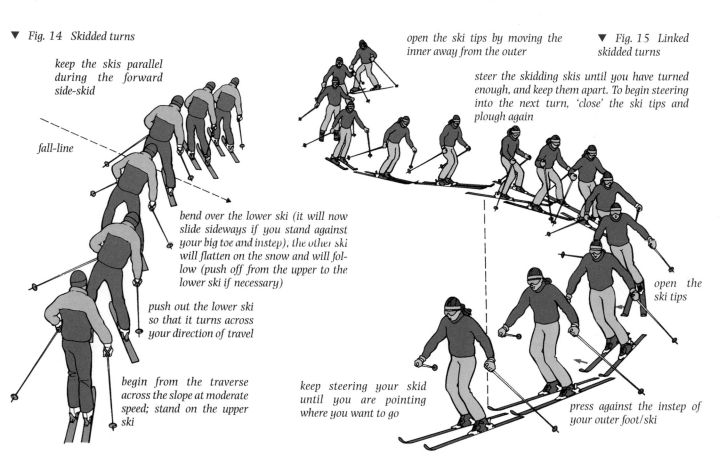

▼ *Fig. 14 Skidded turns*

keep the skis parallel during the forward side-skid

fall-line

bend over the lower ski (it will now slide sideways if you stand against your big toe and instep), the other ski will flatten on the snow and will follow (push off from the upper to the lower ski if necessary)

push out the lower ski so that it turns across your direction of travel

begin from the traverse across the slope at moderate speed; stand on the upper ski

open the ski tips by moving the inner away from the outer

▼ *Fig. 15 Linked skidded turns*

steer the skidding skis until you have turned enough, and keep them apart. To begin steering into the next turn, 'close' the ski tips and plough again

open the ski tips

keep steering your skid until you are pointing where you want to go

press against the instep of your outer foot/ski

29

Finding the route down the mountain

While you are a member of a ski class, your instructor will demonstrate the 'best' way down the mountain. Being off line by as little as a single metre/yard can make descent much more difficult. So make sure that you follow precisely where he leads you, and take the timing of your turns from him.

The golden rule is: go where he goes and turn where he turns.

Sooner or later you will be skilful enough to ski down finding your own route.

First ensure that you are where you want to be by checking your piste map before setting off from the top of the lift. Also check that you are skiing in the right direction by studying the piste markers. You don't want to set off for a blue or red piste only to find yourself at the top of an intimidating black run with no obvious, safer way down. If this happens (and it can often happen in bad visibility), be sensible and walk or side-step back the way you came

until you are able to pin-point your location. If in doubt, ask a lift attendant, a passing instructor or another skier.

When you arrive at the top of your chosen piste, *stop* at the side. Plan a route that will take you 50 m or so to another safe place to stop at the edge of the piste. Visualise exactly where your skis will go. Ski down following as closely as you can your chosen path. Keep repeating this process until you arrive safely at the bottom of the run.

Remember: if a skier below you skis across your intended path and a collision is likely, it is *your* responsibility to avoid him and you *must* change direction. A swing to the hill probably provides the easiest and safest escape route.

On your next run, gradually lengthen the distance between stops but don't be overly ambitious.

When you can travel 100 m/yds each time, change the process; slow down as you approach a chosen point, look down the hill, select a new route and continue down for greater distances without stopping.

Bumps and moguls

Moguls are snow bumps of varying sizes on a piste. Many skiers find them very disconcerting. In fact, moguls can help the skier turn if he uses them correctly.

Learn to ski in moguls by joining the mogul hill near the bottom. Select two or three bumps to cope with first before you attempt to ski down a longer mogul hill or 'mogul field' as they are known.

Aim at a point halfway up the shoulder of a mogul. When your foot reaches that point, close the tip of the uphill ski; at the same time open the tip of the downhill ski and skid around the mogul. Be careful: it is very easy to over-steer because the tips and tails of the skis are not in contact with the snow at the moment the turn is started.

As you become more confident, aim at the bottom third of the mogul, and as you speed up aim to ski in the trough. This is the path of the skiers who made the moguls in the first place.

When you have learnt all the techniques described so far, you will be in possession of a repertoire of techniques that will provide the basis for you to become a skilful skier. How quickly you progress is, of course, dependent on the time you are able to spend on skis. If this time is limited to one or two weeks a year, it will probably take six to ten years before you are able to consider yourself an advanced skier. More skiing and/or expert coaching can reduce this time.

Core form skiing

One of your aims should be to develop rhythmic and fluent, continuously linked arcs. You ski down the fall-line whilst sending your feet and skis out to each side: that is to say your motion is forwards and your movements are sideways. This results in an s-shaped wave-like path called core form skiing, because it is at the 'core' or the heart of all advanced skiing in competition or powder snow.

If you would like to ski more frequently, join a local ski club. Most artificial ski slopes have one or more ski clubs that use the slope as the focal point for their activities. Clubs organise training and coaching sessions for all ages and abilities. Club members who are qualified coaches and instructors are able to give skiers the personal attention and encouragement that will enable them to improve their skiing ability between visits to the snow. Clubs also organise visits to resorts, where their coaching staff are able to continue to work with you.

In addition to the attraction of being able to ski regularly, you will find that most ski clubs have an enjoyable social calendar and are often able to offer discounts to members for the purchase of ski equipment and clothing. If you are interested in becoming a member of a ski club, ask at your local slope, or in the UK contact The English Ski Council for a list of member clubs (see page 2).

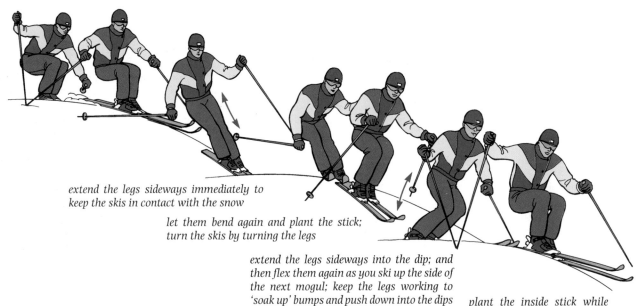

extend the legs sideways immediately to
keep the skis in contact with the snow

let them bend again and plant the stick;
turn the skis by turning the legs

extend the legs sideways into the dip; and
then flex them again as you ski up the side of
the next mogul; keep the legs working to
'soak up' bumps and push down into the dips
while the upper body remains calm and
relaxed

plant the inside stick while
starting to steer the skis

▲ Fig. 16 Mogul skiing

Competitive skiing

Competitive skiing falls into three categories:

- alpine
- nordic
- freestyle.

Alpine racing

Alpine racing has four separate disciplines for men and women.

Slalom

In slalom, competitors race on a steep course marked with alternate pairs of blue and red spring-loaded poles to form 'gates'. If a competitor fails to keep his skis between the poles, he is disqualified. A slalom competition is decided on the aggregate time of two runs, each on a different course.

Slalom requires the competitors to be agile, and possess accurate technique and great confidence. The best skiers achieve speeds in excess of 40 km/h (25 mph).

Giant slalom

In a giant slalom race, the double-pole gates are set wider apart, requiring the skiers to make longer, more rounded turns at speeds in excess of 80 km/h (50 mph).

Super giant slalom

Super giant slalom, or 'Super G', is a cross between giant slalom and downhill racing. There are fewer gates, and as a consequence speeds of up to 115 km/h (70 mph) can be attained.

Downhill

In a downhill race the competitors choose the fastest line on a course marked with widely spaced control gates. The average speed of female competitors is around 70 km/h (45 mph), and of men is 95 km/h (60 mph). Some of the best racers reach speeds of 145 km/h (90 mph) on the fastest sections of the course.

Downhill racing is not accessible to ordinary holiday or club skiers. It requires whole sections of mountains to be closed to the general public. It is also potentially very dangerous because of the great control needed at high speeds. All aspiring downhill racers have to progress through slalom and giant slalom racing into downhill training.

Nordic skiing

'Nordic' is the general term used to describe cross-country skiing. It is a very popular form of the sport, particularly in the Scandinavian countries of Norway, Sweden and Finland, and also in the northern-most territories of the former Soviet Union. In these countries skiing is, of course, not just a sport or a recreation, but remains an important means of transport during the winter months.

Both the equipment and the clothing used by nordic skiers is very different from that of alpine skiers, and is also much less expensive. The skis are longer, narrower and lighter. Many now have a ribbed sole to prevent skiers slipping back down a hill. The bindings are by comparison quite simple, with the toe fastened to the ski, which makes walking far easier but turning more difficult. The ski sticks are almost shoulder height and are used to push the skiers along on the flat. The boots are lightweight, similar to a pair of training shoes. The clothing is also lightweight; because the activity is so energetic, there is no need to be as well insulated from the cold as in high Alpine environments.

Cross-country racing

Cross-country ski racing is similar to cross-country running. The courses are set over similar undulating terrain, without any very long, steep sections. When a course is prepared before a competition, tracks are cut in the snow for the competitors to follow. This ensures that everyone has similar conditions. The distances of international races vary from 10 km (6 miles) for women, up to as far as 50 km (30 miles) for men.

Biathlon

In a biathlon nordic event, each competitor carries a light rifle and ammunition while they ski a loop course. They stop at a shooting range several times to fire five shots at a target. Missing the target translates into a time penalty.

Ski jumping

Ski jump competitors are arguably among the most courageous of all sportspeople. Travelling at over 80 km/h (50 mph), they jump from a ramp and achieve distances of over 100 m (110 yds). In addition to the distance jumped, style marks are awarded that contribute to deciding the winner.

Ski jumps may be built in the snow, or covered by artificial ski slope surface for use all the year round. The size and shape of the jumping hill will give a maximum safe distance that normally can be achieved on that hill. These are designated at 25 m (27 yds) or 30 m (33 yds) on learning hills, and at 70 m (76 yds) or 90 m (98 yds) on hills for international and Olympic competitions.

Ski jumpers use very long skis – over 230 cm (90 in) in length – which are very broad and very heavy.

Freestyle skiing

Freestyle skiing is a comparatively recent development within the sport. It uses short alpine skis.

Ski acrobatics

'Ski acro' is similar in its form to ice skating. Competitors perform a series of linked jumps, spins and gliding movements, to music, on a shallow piste.

Moguls

Mogul competitions involve skiers descending a steep, moguled slope at speed, having to perform a number of aerial stunts during the run.

Aerials

Competitors take off from a ramp and perform twists and somersaults, similar to those of trampolinists, before landing.

To compete

Join a club. When you can ski well enough you can enter competitions. Alternatively, you can register with your governing body and enter competitions graded according to your ability and your national 'seeding'.

British Alpine Ski Awards

In the UK, even if you don't wish to race, you can still 'compete' against yourself and measure your progress by achieving one or more of the five awards that make up the British Alpine Ski Awards. One star is awarded to novices, five stars to real experts.

For further information about the awards scheme, the national racing and freestyle competition structures, and the national squads, contact the governing body for the sport, the English Ski Council (*see* page 2).

Snowboarding

Introduction

The sport of snowboarding began in 1965 when Sherman Poppen invented 'the Snurfer' by bolting two skis together. This was followed by Bob Webber's 'Skiboard' design in 1972, and the first National Snowboarding Championships were held at Snow Valley, Vermont, USA, in 1983. Finally, in November 1996 the International Olympic Committee accepted snowboarding as an official medal discipline for the 1998 Olympic Games in Nagano, Japan.

The British Snowboard Association was founded in 1988 to gather together the increasing number of snowboarders in Britain in order to improve communication between them and also improve all aspects of the sport.

The British Snowboard Association (marketing information)

4 Cross Road
Oxhey
Hertfordshire
WD1 4DH

Tel/fax: 01923 228812
E-mail: bsaengland@aol.com

Equipment

Your local snowboard retailer will be able to offer sound, unbiased advice about equipment, and show you a selection of boards, boots, bindings and clothing to suit all needs and pockets.

Snowboards

There are many snowboards on the market today. All share the same basic shape and qualities: wide at the nose (front), narrow down to the waist (middle section), and widening again towards the tail (back). Generally they are divided into three different types.

Freeride snowboards

These are the most popular snowboards, and the majority fall within this category. They can cope with all types of riding and all types of terrain and are used by both beginner and expert alike as they combine the best of both freestyle and carving board elements.

Freestyle snowboards

These are used by riders who perform the stunning acrobatic manoeuvres off jumps and in the 'halfpipe' (*see* page 43). In general, freestyle snowboards (*see* page 39) are wider and stiffer than the freeride models so that the rider has a strong platform off which to leap to perform the trick. The feet are also positioned so that the rider can spin the board around easily.

Carving snowboards

These are used by riders who are competing on the race circuit, as well as those who prefer to ride on hard, flat pistes. They offer a chance to ride faster than either freeride or freestyle boards as they are finely tuned and are narrower over the whole length than other types of snowboard.

The following guidelines will also help you select the most appropriate snowboard.

• The length and stiffness of your board will largely be determined by your height and weight. Someone of average weight and around 170 cm (5 ft 8 in) in height will probably use a 154 cm board. As a general rule, the heavier the individual, the stiffer the board needed.

• Skill level also determines the required stiffness of the board. If you are a first-season rider you will probably be happier with a softer board as this will enable you to make turns more easily. A stiffer board can be adopted as you start to 'carve' and make more aggressive turns.

Boots and bindings

Unlike ski boots, you do not need to change into a pair of moonboots for the après-ski activities. Snowboard boots are very comfortable, and you should base your choice on whichever pair feels best on your feet.

The binding – the mechanism that offers support to your feet and legs – generally comes with two base plates (fixings) to suit the type of board that you have. A medium-height binding will suit the needs of most snowboarders.

However, the so-called 'step-in' has been developed recently. This combines snowboard boot comfort with ski boot-type fixings, allowing the rider to attach himself to the snowboard much faster than if he was using the conventional boot/binding system shown opposite. The choice is vast, and two rules apply when making your choice – comfort and budget.

Clothing

The sport of snowboarding has been a major influence on the fashion industry during the last few years, and ordinary winterwear has been dominated by technical clothing. This means that you can go to many high street retail chains and buy suitable snowboard clothing at a fraction of the cost of several years ago.

Basic skills

Below is a guide to the basic skills of snowboarding, along with some useful exercises to assist your learning. In addition, visit your local artificial slope and ask for lessons from a British Snowboard Association instructor.

Stance

In the search for the perfect snowboard stance a good starting point is to assume the position of the 'goalkeeper' waiting to save a penalty. Body weight should be centred, knees bent (ready to absorb bumps or allow you to push into the air from a jump), and hands at mid-thigh level. From this position the rider can cope with any change in snow condition or terrain.

Balance

Balance is an essential part of snowboarding. Exercises to ensure good balance are used throughout the teaching process, and once learned on the dry slope are easily transferred on to snow. However, anyone who has a grasp of other board sports (either skate or surf) will automatically have a keen sense of balance.

Edge control

Whilst on the flat of the slope, position your hands on your hips and push your hips forwards so that they are over the toeside edge of the board. Raise your heels and balance on your toes.

Once you can do this, you will find that you need to exert less pressure to gain good edge control when on the slope. This exercise also helps with balance.

Weight distribution

Again, practise on the flat. Whilst strapped into the board and in the basic stance, keep your upper body straight and shift your weight over your front foot. Keep adding weight until the tail (back) of the board raises off the ground.

Repeat the exercise with your rear foot, this time raising the board's nose (front). This will help build your confidence and show just how much weight can be shifted across the board.

Simple manoeuvres

Sidestep

Place your front foot in the binding and push off with your back foot. Keep the toe edge of the board in contact with the snow to ensure a good grip. This technique allows you to move along the flat and uphill, which is useful for crossing over to the lift queue in a resort.

Straight run

This is usually the first movement you will try with both feet strapped to the snowboard. Adopt a comfortable basic stance (balanced and with your weight equally distributed), and then travel a short distance on a flat, shallow slope.

Sideslip

Once you have mastered the straight run, turn the board parallel to the slope and use the uphill edge to dig into the snow to act as a brake. The more pressure exerted on to the edge, the greater the braking action. This manoeuvre forms the basis of all stopping exercises.

Diagonal sideslip

This is similar to the sideslip, but your weight is now shifted on to one foot. This makes the board travel sideways across the slope and also downhill, whilst still using a braking motion.

Falling leaf

This is a continuation of the diagonal sideslip. Whilst travelling sideways across the slope, take your weight off your leading foot so that you are centred again with the board travelling momentarily downhill (with the braking motion intact). Shift your weight on to the other foot to travel diagonally downwards in the other direction.

Garland

The garland is a series of partial turns. Start off with a sideslip, and add weight to the leading foot until the board starts to point downhill. By releasing the weight and pressure the board returns to its sideways travel. Repeat this several times and you will make a series of 'J' shapes in the snow behind you. The movement feels similar to a true turn.

Making the turn

Once you have worked through the basic skills you will be ready to make a turn. Many beginners freeze at this point because it involves travelling with the board's nose pointing straight downhill for a short time – entering and then crossing the fall-line (*see* page 14). The move also involves a new element: changing edges. This means that you end up facing the opposite direction of travel when the turn is completed.

- From the basic stance, add weight to the front foot so that you begin a diagonal sideslip. This will automatically start to move the board across the slope.
- Start to flatten your feet, lessening the pressure exerted on the uphill edge so that the board points downhill.
- Taking care not to panic, carry on until you feel the edge change on the board. When the downhill edge bites into the snow, the board will steer across the snow, completing an arc. You have mastered your first turn.

Successful completion of a series of turns means that all of the skills learned throughout the initial exercises have been employed. The next stage is to practise the turns until they become fluid movements.

Additional exercises at this point involve:

- co-ordination – linking turns and body movements
- rhythm – to keep turns fluid throughout changes in terrain and snow conditions (such as steep or icy sections)
- control of speed – to ensure that you are able to keep a speed check on the snowboard at all times, even under difficult conditions
- control of line – to ensure that you are able to assess the best and safest route down the mountain, avoiding all obstacles.

Advanced skills

As soon as most snowboarders can link two turns they crave for something else: air. This section gives tips on how to leave the ground safely.

The approach to a jump is very important and should incorporate comfort, balance and stability. Let the curve of the jump take you into the air, but if this is your first attempt, don't worry about gaining extra height just yet!

Initially, you may grab the board with a tentative touch or stroke. However, as you become more confident, you will be able to stay in the air long enough to make full contact with the board. You can then try some of the more recognised snowboarding tricks.

The indy

This is the most common snowboarding trick, and is the easiest to learn. Whilst in the air, pull your knees up and, with the rear hand, grab the toe-side edge of the board between your feet.

The mute grab

Whilst bending the knees, move your front hand across your body. Grab the board between your feet on the toeside edge.

The tail grab

This trick is fairly easy yet looks very stylish. As the name suggests, grab the tail of the board whilst in the air and hold on to it for as long as possible.

The nose grab

Once again the name gives this away. This is an old trick, but it is still stylish in a big jump. Whilst in the air, bring the front hand to the nose of the board and pull it up, bending the front leg for effect.

Other techniques

Nowadays nearly all resort areas cater for snowboarders. The better ones have built special parks where snowboarders can spend all day honing their freestyle skills. These usually contain various jumps or 'hits' of differing sizes to suit all levels, from the beginner to the advanced rider. The more established parks also have full halfpipe facilities – huge channels gouged from the snow by 'pipe dragons' (heavy plant machinery that has been adapted to cut a perfect semicircular shape into the snow to enable riders to perform tricks).

However, advanced snowboarding skills are not soley the property of freestyle riders. Many riders are happiest when there has been a fresh snowfall – the time when snowboarders really get to express themselves.

Phase 4 – the rider should be at the optimum height and the trick should be held or styled

Phase 5 – the trick should have been released and the rider starts to prepare for the landing and aligns the body

Phase 3 – the rider starts the execution of the chosen trick. The body finishes releasing the stored energy

Phase 6 – the rider is just about to touch down. The posture should be perfectly balanced and aligned, ready to absorb the landing

Phase 2 – the rider is at the top of the jump, attempting to gain maximum height

Phase 7 – the rider should make a solid landing, the upcoming ground absorbed by compressing the legs

▲ *Fig. 17 The phases of a snowboard trick*

Phase 1 – the rider approaches the hit. Good posture is needed: crouch down and absorb the power for the manoeuvre

Big turns

In untouched snowfields, these are akin to surfing and it's easy to see the similarities. The biggest percentage of snowboarders are 'freeriders', which means they tackle all mountain conditions and are able to utilise on- and off-piste skills.

Carving

This is part of the riding process and involves manoeuvres and edge changes carried out on the piste at high speed. It is a difficult style to master and is best suited to hard-boot setups (mostly used in slalom and competition, *see* page 47).

Back country

Back country riding is a rapidly growing facet of the sport. It involves riders being kitted up for long walks away from the piste areas, and covering untracked ground using snowshoes. It is a highly dangerous area of snowboarding and should only be undertaken in the company of a qualified mountain guide. Riders could easily get lost in the vast wooded areas surrounding resorts or possibly encounter one of the crevasses that are present in nearly all mountain regions.

Heliboarding

This is the ultimate in snowboarding: a trip to the top of the mountain area in a helicopter. Riders are set down on perfect, untouched snow and are guided down through spectacular scenery by the mountain guide. Reserved only for those who are able to afford such a luxury!

Competitive snowboarding

Once you have mastered the basic snowboarding skills you may wish to find an arena in which to express them. Many riders are simply happy to freeride on the open mountain, but others need to pit their skills against fellow boarders on the competitive scene.

There is a large competitive series in the UK. The British Snowboard Association's National Points Series is held on artificial surfaces throughout the country between May and November. Riders compete in both slalom and freestyle events and their scores are tallied to produce winners in all age categories. The standard of riding is outstanding, many of the riders having learned their trade at the dry slope 'club nights' where top local riders coach the juniors and up-and-coming competitors.

The next step is to transfer these skills to the snow and move on to the British Snowboard Association

Championships held annually in Europe. These include four disciplines – slalom, boardercross, halfpipe and big-air – the points scored in each being added together to find the overall British Champion.

Slalom

Two riders race across a set course of slalom poles, swap lanes and then race again. The runs are timed and the two times combined to give a total. The top 16 riders then race again head-to-head in a knockout to find the winner.

Boardercross

Four or six riders race down one course over bumps, jumps and bends in an attempt to cross the finish line first. The top riders in each round go through to the next round until there are a final four, who then compete head-to-head.

Halfpipe

Riders demonstrate freestyle skills in the huge channel described on page 43. The riders are allowed two runs down it to impress the judges, who score them on the quality of each run.

Big-air

Each rider travels airborne off a large specially-constructed jump. They perform tricks mid-air and are judged on the difficulty of the trick and the height gained.

Index